Introduc

Llandrindod Wells, the county town c and Edwardian buildings, as well as gardens. A network of recently improved r connecting with the beauty spots of Cefnllys and Alpine Bridge, the woodlands to the east and north of the town, the remains of the largest Roman fort in Wales (Castell Collen) and across the hill to the nearby village of Howey.

Walking routes also connect Llandrindod Wells with some of the other towns and villages in the area. Builth Wells, the home of the Royal Welsh Agricultural Show, can be reached by a varied 10 mile walk that includes the Carneddau Hills. There are also walks around Builth Wells and the hills to the south, with one route on firm surfaces throughout.

Another route from Llandrindod Wells leads to Newbridge-on-Wye, around and near which there are a number of circular routes to be explored, including one that makes use of part of the Wye Valley Walk. The village of Llanwrthwl, between Newbridge-on-Wye and Rhayader, provides the starting point for two circular walks, one of which combines the Wye Valley Walk with part of Abergwesyn Common.

A route leads from the village of Llanyre (across the valley from Llandrindod Wells) to Rhayader with the option of shortening this walk using a bus service about one mile from the course of the walk.

A network of local buses, plus the scenic Heart of Wales Railway Line, connects Llandrindod Wells to the places mentioned in this guide. In addition to the walks to Builth Wells, Newbridge-on-Wye and Rhayader already mentioned, a bus service to Llandegley leads to the start of a linear walk back to Llandrindod Wells.

Each walk includes a map and directions, enabling the route to be followed without difficulty. Footpaths and bridleways are frequently waymarked, particularly near the towns and villages. When crossing open access land (where a number of parallel routes can exist) a suggested route is included. Details of Powys bus service numbers are included in the information for particular walks, where relevant. The Powys Travel Guide is available free from Llandrindod Wells Tourist Information Centre and from Powys County Council. This provides comprehensive details of public transport at the time of its publication – walkers are advised to check with service operators if planning to catch a bus in a rural location.

The use of walking boots and suitable clothing for walks contained in this guide is recommended. Please check weather forecasts, particularly if you are following upland paths. The location of each walk and its starting point is shown inside the covers, together with approximate walking times. Allow extra time if exploring places of interest on the routes. Please follow The Country Code and – *enjoy your walking*!

WALK I
AROUND BUILTH WELLS

DESCRIPTION Two linked walks at Builth Wells, one moderate and one easy, which can be combined. The moderate walk follows a bridleway through woodland and then descends to a riverside path on the way back to town. The easy walk follows the Rivers Wye and Irfon and, with a shortening of the route, would be suitable for wheelchair users. Allow about 1½ hours for the moderate route and about 1¼ hours for the easy route.

START The Groe car park, Builth Wells, SO 043511.

MODERATE ROUTE (2¾ miles)

I From the roadside near the Black Bull statue, head up towards the Wye Bridge. Cross the bridge and cross the main road with care. Follow the track to the right of Wyeside Furnishers and continue AHEAD. Go through a waymarked gate to the right of the Jewson building and continue along the track and then the tarmac path. When the tarmac path veers right towards a waymarked gate, turn LEFT and head for a small gate leading onto the main road.

2 Turn RIGHT and follow the main road to the junction of the A483 and A481. Follow the right hand verge of the A483 (Llandrindod Wells road) for a few yards,

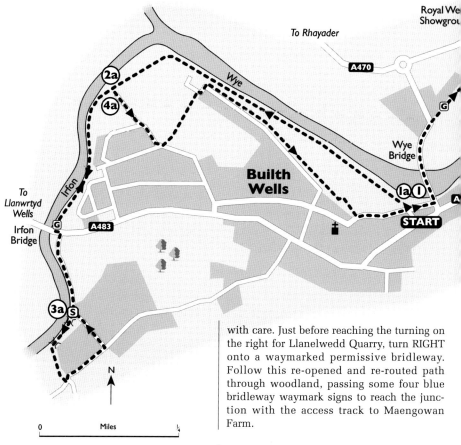

with care. Just before reaching the turning on the right for Llanelwedd Quarry, turn RIGHT onto a waymarked permissive bridleway. Follow this re-opened and re-routed path through woodland, passing some four blue bridleway waymark signs to reach the junction with the access track to Maengowan Farm.

2

3 Turn RIGHT and follow the access track downhill. Go right at the fork in the track, soon coming to the junction with the A481. Cross the main road with care and enter the side road opposite, leading to Wyeside Enterprise Park, Follow the road through the trading estate and round to the left. At a crossroads, continue AHEAD and then follow the lane round to the right. Soon bear HALF LEFT on the waymarked cycleway.

3 a Follow the path alongside the Irfon, crossing another footbridge and then bearing LEFT and RIGHT to reach a lane. Turn LEFT on the lane and LEFT at the next junction. Follow the road to the first turning on the left (Irfon Bridge Road). Turn into this and follow it back past the start of the footpath to the kissing gate and steps. Return along the riverside path to the path junction near the footbridge crossed by the Wye Valley Walk.

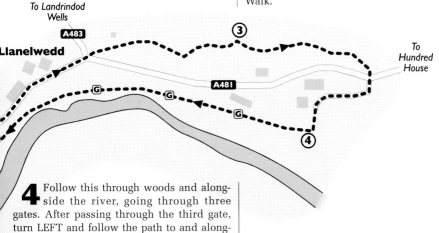

To Landrindod Wells

A483

Llanelwedd

(3)

To Hundred House

A481

G G G

(4)

garth

4 Follow this through woods and alongside the river, going through three gates. After passing through the third gate, turn LEFT and follow the path to and alongside the Jewson building. Go through another gate and continue AHEAD to the road. Head LEFT over the Wye Bridge and turn RIGHT to return to the Groe.

EASY ROUTE (2½ miles)

I a Follow the riverside path alongside the Wye, on the course of the Wye Valley Walk – look out for the carving of the Leaping Salmon (the symbol of this long distance route). At the junction of the Wye and Irfon, turn LEFT and continue along the tarmac path to reach a footbridge.

2 a Do not cross the footbridge but continue AHEAD* on a grassy path. Follow this to and up steps to a kissing gate onto a road. Cross the road with care and enter Irfon Bridge Road opposite. Follow the road past metal and then wooden railings on the right. When the road bends to the left, follow a waymarked path HALF RIGHT to a footbridge and stile.

4 a Turn RIGHT and follow the tarmac path and then the lane to the junction with a road. Bear LEFT on the road. Pass a turning on the right and soon afterwards, turn LEFT on a tarmac path leading across the edge of the playing fields on the left. Pass ornate gates off to the right, and shortly afterwards, turn RIGHT on a tarmac path running parallel to the Wye Valley Walk route followed on the outward journey. Follow this path back to the Groe, passing near the National Eisteddfod Stone Circle.

* For the wheelchair accessible route, turn LEFT onto the tarmac path at this point and follow the main route as set out in stage 4a.

AROUND CEFNLLYS

DESCRIPTION This is a moderate walk of about 3½ miles around a local beauty spot. Highlights include a mediaeval church, the hill top site of a marcher castle, woodland and riverside nature reserve and a circular walk along both sides of an attractive valley. Allow about 2 hours for this route.

START Roadside parking area near Shaky Bridge, SO 0846 12.

I From the parking area, follow the road back to a gate on the right, beyond which is a footbridge over the Ithon. Cross the bridge and take the footpath leading HALF LEFT to a kissing gate into the churchyard. When ready to leave the churchyard, exit by the main gate and go STRAIGHT AHEAD across the field to a gate onto the open access area. Turn LEFT on the track and follow this until approaching the house (Neuadd). At this point, turn SHARP RIGHT and head uphill to the summit of Castle Bank (site of a marcher castle with excellent views).

2 When ready, retrace the outward route downhill, LEFT along the track and RIGHT through the gate. Head towards the church for a few yards, then turn LEFT and follow a path between two rows of trees and then across open ground to the footbridge. Once through the gate, turn RIGHT through a small gate and follow the path through Bailey Einon Nature Reserve. On reaching a fork in the boardwalk section, take either route (these join in due course). On reaching a gate, turn and retrace the outward route back to the road.

3 Turn RIGHT and follow the road towards Llandrindod Wells. When the road begins to climb steeply, go through a waymarked gate set back to the left. Follow the track along the left-hand side of a field, through a gate and then follow the track round to the right. Continue to follow the track along the side of the valley (look out for the entrances to a small area of woodland with permissive access, on the right). Go through a waymarked gate, past the turning for Upper Llanoley and along the track to a lane.

4 Turn LEFT on the lane. At the end of the lane continue AHEAD on a track until reaching a waymarked stile on the left, shortly before a gate across the track. Cross the stile and follow the path ahead, through a waymarked gate. Continue to follow the path AHEAD through woodland and then across an open area to a kissing gate into conifers. Follow the path AHEAD through the conifers to reach the road near the parking area.

Bailey-Einon Wood

To Landrindod Wells

Cefnllys

Castle Bank

Shaky Bridge

START

Upper Llanoley

N

0   Miles   ¼

WALK 3

CAERHYDDWEN FOREST

DESCRIPTION A circular route near Llanwrthwl, some 3¼ miles to the south of Rhayader, near the A470. This moderate walk of about 5 miles includes some striking views of the Wye Valley from an area of open access hill land. A café/shop and the Vulcan Arms are located a short distance from the route. Parking is available in roadside lay-bys and, to a limited extent, by the church in Llanwrthwl village. Car park areas at the café/shop and public house are for patrons. Allow about 3 hours for the walk.

START A470 at the turning for Llanwrthwl village, SN 977640.

PUBLIC TRANSPORT Powys bus service 47 passes along the A470.

I Follow the main road south, until reaching the turning for Nant-glas, on the left. Head along the minor road (*look out for the entrance to the Living Willow Theatre on the left – details about this can be obtained at www.livingwillowtheatre. co.uk or by phoning 01597 811487*). Continue along the road, passing St Mark's Church near Yr Hsfa (*those who have read 'Kilvert's Diary' may remember that the Victorian cleric/walker was present at the start of construction and the consecration of the church*). Ignore the footpath sign on the left and continue for a short way further to reach a bridleway gate on the left.

2 Go through the gate and follow the bridleway through Caerhyddwen Forest. At the first junction of tracks, turn RIGHT on the permissive route (white footprint on

blue background). Follow the track ahead and then round to the left – some good hill views on route. On returning to the bridleway, turn RIGHT. Cross a turning area and then a bridge. Just after the bridge, take the right fork at the two-way bridleway sign. Follow the track uphill and through the trees. Shortly after joining another track coming from the right, go through a gate on the right into the open access area.

3 Follow the clear route AHEAD through the bracken, allowing excellent views over the hills around the Wye valley at this spot. On coming in sight of the Wye, down to the right, follow sheep paths and tracks down hill in that direction. On reaching a wide path at the base of the hill, turn LEFT and follow this to a gate roughly in the middle of the area of open access land (this shortens the length of road walking needed to reach Llanwrthl turn). Go through the gate, turn LEFT and follow the main road verge with care to reach the turn for Llanwrthl in about ½ to ¾ mile.

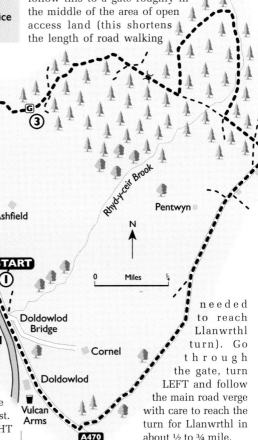

5

WALK 4

CASTELL COLLEN, LLANFIHANGEL HELYGEN & LLANYRE

DESCRIPTION A 6½ mile walk, with attractive views throughout. The route goes from Llandrindod Wells town centre by cyclepath/footpath, quiet road and lane to Castell Collen Roman Fort. The walk then follows a footpath route to the church at Llanfihangel Helygen, before following a lane and footpath to Llanyre. From here, the cycling/walking route can be followed back to Llandrindod Wells or a bus caught from Llanyre. Allow about 4 hours for the walk.

START Railway Station/bus stops/car park in central Llandrindod Wells, SO 059614.

PUBLIC TRANSPORT Llandrindod Wells is on the Heart of Wales line and has a number of bus services. Llanyre is on Powys bus service route 47 between Newbridge-on-Wye and Llandrindod Wells.

1 From the 'up platform' of Railway Station (the opposite side from the Booking Office), head towards the large car park. Cross the road to the 19th century red brick building (currently the Police Station and Magistrates' Court). Follow Dyffryn Road down the left hand side of this building Ignore the first two footpath signs on the right and follow the road past the entrance to the High School and Sports Centre. Just beyond these buildings, turn RIGHT onto a waymarked cycling/walking path. Follow this until reaching the entrance to a housing estate. Continue AHEAD on Holcombe Avenue and then turn RIGHT into Holcombe Drive. At the t-junction, turn LEFT and follow the road down to the junction with the main road.

2 Join the cycling/walking route on the right and follow this across the Llanyre Bridge. Follow the path to the RIGHT and

then go up steps to a stile on the right. Keep to the right of the enclosure fence and then bear HALF LEFT to reach a stile onto a lane. Turn RIGHT in the lane and follow this past 'Cwm' on the left. Continue along the lane, looking out for a small information board about the Roman Fort and a permissive path sign, both on the right. Follow the permissive route through a gate on the right and head along the right hand side of the field to reach a waymarked gate into the area of the Roman Fort (now a permissive open access area). Turn RIGHT and walk around the large fort *(occupied between the 1st and 4th centuries AD)*.

3 When ready, return to the lane and turn RIGHT. Follow the lane to the point where this bends sharply to the right. At this point, follow the footpath waymarking signs through a gate directly ahead (i.e. do not join the bridleway on the left) and take the left hand footpath, heading HALF LEFT across the field to a stile into a wooded area. Cross a small stream and continue HALF LEFT to exit the trees and cross the field to a waymarked gate. Head slightly to the right across the next field, passing a waymark sign on fencing on route, to reach a stile. Cross and then follow the right hand boundary of a third field to reach a gate onto a road.

4 Turn RIGHT and follow the road for a short way to a waymarked gate on the left (just before Castell-Gwynt on the right). Cross the field, passing just to the left of a pile of stones, to a gate by a hedge on the right. Continue along the right hand side of the field and then SLIGHTLY TO THE LEFT to reach a stile. Go HALF LEFT across the next field and pass through a line of trees that marks an old field boundary (by a clump of trees on the right). Follow the fenceline on the right to reach a stile into the ground of St Michael in the Willows Church – which has box pews (not original to this site), an 11th century font and a 14th century roof.

5 When ready, leave the church grounds via the main gate and turn LEFT along the lane (passing benches on the left that provide a scenic place to take a break). Cross

Pentre Bach Bridge. Turn RIGHT at the junction with a smaller lane, opposite Bryn-bedwen. Continue along the lane until reaching the end of the third field on the left. Pass through a gate set back on the left and follow the track through a narrow waymarked gate and along the right hand side of a narrow field. Just beyond the next waymarked

6 Turn LEFT and follow the track to the junction with the road through Llanyre. Turn RIGHT to follow the road through the village to the church (on the left) and the Bell Inn (on the right). The latter originally dates from the 17th century. This section of the route leads past Llanyre Hall (by a road junction on the left) and the Pritchard Recreation Ground – *a wooded area containing a short walk, also on the left.*

7 When you are ready to leave Llanyre*, retrace your steps to the turning by Llanyre Hall. Turn RIGHT here and follow the lane to the junction with the main road. Turn LEFT on the cycling/walking route and follow this towards Llandrindod Wells. Shortly after crossing the Llanyre Bridge, cross the main road with care to a stile on the right and follow the footpath HALF LEFT across two fields, connected by a gate. Cross a final stile to rejoin the main road, cross with care and head RIGHT along the pavement. On reaching the junction with Dyffryn Road (on the left), turn LEFT and follow the road back past the High School to the corner by the Magistrates' Court.

✱ *If wishing to shorten the walk, a bus can be caught back from Llanyre, at the bus stop on the road between Llanyre Hall and the Bell Inn.*

gate, head HALF LEFT to a stile – *traditional hedge laying has taken place here.* Follow the left hand side of the field to the next stile and then head across the middle of the next field to a further stile. Cross and head SLIGHTLY TO THE LEFT to reach a stile in a dip. Cross the stile and a small stream and climb the bank to a stile onto a track.

CASTLE BANK CIRCULAR

DESCRIPTION A walk of either 6 or 10 miles, following a circular mainly upland route around open access land with a wide range of excellent views. The route passes the site of an old hill fort and includes some rough walking, but is never very far from a minor road. Allow 4 or 6 hours for the walk.

START Roadside parking by the Howey to Hundred House road, at SO 080569 OR bus stops at the Howey Village turn. SO 052588.

PUBLIC TRANSPORT Howey is on the main bus route between Llandrindod Wells and Builth Wells – there are various services, including TrawsCambria Brecon to Newtown. The walk is some two miles from the nearest bus route at Howey Village, but the consistently good views make it well worth the effort of following the minor road to get there. See the Powys Travel Guide, available from Llandrindod Wells Tourist Information Centre.

I *From the roadside parking place*, follow the road towards Howey, until just before the cattle grid. Turn LEFT to follow the boundary wall on the right around two small hills, *affording views towards the Carneddau Hills.*

From Howey Village turn bus stop, follow the road south to the Hundred House turning and then turn LEFT along this minor road (the course of an old Drover's Route from Newbridge-on-Wye to Kington, just over the border in England) for about two miles. After crossing a cattle grid, bear RIGHT to follow the boundary wall on the right around two small hills, affording views towards the Carneddau hills.

2 On completing the turn around the back of the second hill, follow a track that leads back toward the road. Just before reaching the road, turn RIGHT on another track that leads downhill, passing to the right of an enclosed area. Continue ahead and climb Castle Bank to the site of the old hill fort. As well as looking at the view from the summit, follow the circular path around the top of this long hill. When ready, head back down towards the road and follow this to the right and over the bridge to a lane (leading to Bettws).

To H
& bu
1½

3 Follow the unfenced lane until approaching the end of the open access area to the left. At this point, turn LEFT onto a path that runs alongside the field boundary, giving access to new views including of a previously hidden valley to the north. Continue alongside this boundary, using a mixture of tracks and sheep paths, until reaching a track by a gate signposted for Upper Gilwern. (The low-lying parts of this section can be wet and it may be necessary to temporarily divert to the left when passing through these).

4 Turn LEFT on the track and follow this back towards the road, passing a cottage on the way – this section of the route provides an excellent opportunity to look back over the ground covered during the circuit. On reaching the road, return to the parking place or turn RIGHT and retrace your steps to the Howey Village turn bus stop.

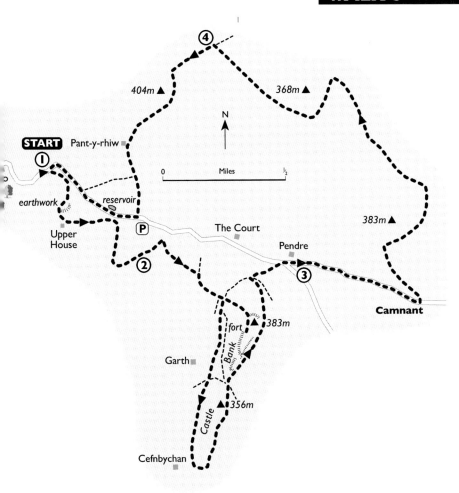

404m ▲

368m ▲

N
↑

START ① Pant-y-rhiw ■

0   Miles   ½

earthwork   reservoir

Upper
House   ℗   The Court

383m ▲

Pendre

②   ③   Camnant

fort ▲ 383m

Garth ■   ▲ 356m

Cefnbychan ■

Castle Bank

CORS Y LLYN
National Nature Reserve

DESCRIPTION An easy walk, with Disabled Access, of about 1 mile, around a National Nature Reserve. The route is composed of level grassy paths and a boardwalk (with two passing places). The reserve (once filmed by Sir David Attenborough) consists of an overgrown lake (across which a boardwalk has been laid) and adjoining fields. The main part of the reserve is approached by a meadow in which over 100 species of flowering plants have been identified – butterflies, including Peacocks and Red Admirals, have been seen here. There is also an area of open water with populations of dragonflies and damselflies, moorhens and amphibians.

Within the main part of the reserve, the boardwalk leads across two contrasting areas of mire, the first the less acidic of the two. A belt of wet woodland surrounds this part of the reserve and is home to a variety of woodland birds, as well as spring and winter visitors. Allow 1-1¼ hours for the walk. See www.ccw.gov.uk for additional details of the reserve.

START Parking area near entrance to Cors y Llyn, SO 016556.

PUBLIC TRANSPORT Powys bus service 47 passes along the Builth Wells to Newbridge-on-Wye road, about ½ mile from the reserve entrance.

1 From the parking area, go through the gate and follow the path along the right hand edge of the field. At the next set of gates, continue along the right hand side of the field to reach the entrance to the boardwalk section of the reserve. Follow the boardwalk (IT IS IMPORTANT TO KEEP TO THE BOARDWALK ON THIS SECTION OF THE ROUTE – SEE SAFETY NOTICES AT THE ENTRANCE TO THE RESERVE), taking the right fork at the junction of routes, to reach the seating area at the far end.

2 When ready, retrace the first part of the outward route to the junction of boardwalk paths. Turn RIGHT and follow the boardwalk to the gate. Beyond the gate, turn LEFT and follow the grassy path to the junction of gates passed on route from the parking area. Turn RIGHT to return to the reserve entrance.

Cors y Llyn

WALK 7

CRAIG CHWEFRI CIRCULAR

DESCRIPTION A hill walk of about 4 miles, on part of Abergwesyn Common (extensive moorland owned by the National Trust). This walk crosses high ground on a relatively dry section of the Common and has extensive hill views as well as views over the Chwefri and Hirnant valleys. The Red Lion at nearby Llanafan-fawr (about 1 mile south on the B4358) is 'the oldest pub in Powys'. Allow about 2½ hours for the walk.

START Unfenced lane leading off from the B4358 about 1 mile north of Llanafan-fawr, SN 975577.

1 Follow the lane to the end of the tarmac section. Turn LEFT on the bridleway running up to the saddle between Lan Fach and Craig Chwefri. On reaching fairly level ground, turn LEFT and head up to the top of the Lan Fach ridge. Take a roughly circular route around Lan Fach and Lan Ganol, then descend back to the lower section of the ridge. (*The remains of Bellitalgarth consists of a pile of stones visible on route*).

2 Cross the lower ground and follow a path running uphill towards the top of Craig Chwefri. On reaching the high ground, take a circular route around the high ground on Craig Chwefri and Llethr Melyn, passing the trig point on Craig Chwefri. Follow the path back down to the lower ground and head LEFT back down to the lane. Turn RIGHT to return to parking place.

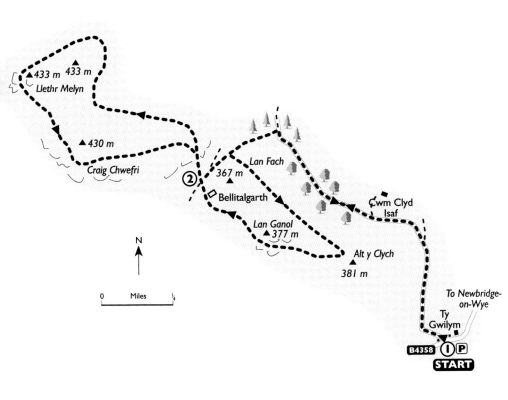

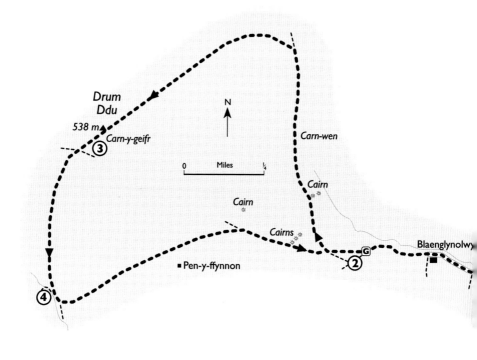

Drum
Ddu
538 m
Carn-y-geifr
③

N

Carn-wen

0   Miles   ¼

Cairn

Cairn

Cairns

G   Blaenglynolwyn

■ Pen-y-ffynnon   ②

④

2 Follow the track AHEAD, with enclosed fields on the right. On coming to a junction of tracks, take the track on tho right. Keep roughly parallel to the fence on the right until this veers right. Then continue STRAIGHT AHEAD across open ground for about 3⁄4 of a mile until coming in sight of the valley at Rhos Cilcolgwm, on the left. Turn away from the wet area of this valley and head LEFT up the hill, keeping an eye out for a path running along the ridge. Join this and follow it AHEAD to reach the cairn and shelter at Carn-y-geifr on Drum Ddu.

1 Take the Beulah road (B4358) from Newbridge-on-Wye, parking on the verge just beyond the Wye Bridge. Cross the main road and follow the minor road past Llysdinam on the left, as it climbs gradually through parkland, then a mixture of fields and woods until reaching views of the surrounding hills. On reaching a crossroads, where the National Cycleway turns right, continue AHEAD on the lane. Pass Blaenglynolwyn Farm and continue AHEAD on the bridleway, which leads through a gate onto Abergwesyn Common, open access land owned by the National Trust.

3 When ready, continue along the path running to the left of Carn-y-geifr, aiming for a rock outcropping visible further along the ridge. On route, pass in sight of a small pond off to the left. Just beyond the outcropping, turn SHARP LEFT and follow a path that shows signs of being used by horse riders. Follow this downhill and HALF RIGHT, keeping to the left of damp ground (farmland soon becomes visible ahead and at one point there is a white-topped marker post some distance off to the right). In due course, reach a track leading down to a ford on the right.

4 DO NOT CROSS THE FORD but turn LEFT away from it and follow a mixture of paths and tracks along the open hill, keeping above the bracken line on the right. Pass to the left of a small area of enclosed land. At the end of the enclosed area, follow a track leading downhill and HALF RIGHT. Continue to descend in this direction until reaching a further area of enclosed fields, where a track leads to the right towards Blaenglynolwyn Farm. Pass the farm and follow the road back to the Beulah road.

WALK 8

DRUM DDU CIRCULAR

DESCRIPTION A moderate 8 mile walk by lane and track onto the eastern section of the National Trust property of Abergwesyn Common. The walk crosses open moorland, visiting the cairn and shelter on Drum Ddu before returning by a different route. The route includes a range of excellent hill views and aims to keep to drier sections of this moorland expanse. THIS WALK USES DRIER SECTIONS OF THE COMMON – WALKERS ARE ADVISED TO AVOID THE WETTER AREAS. Allow about 4¾ hours for the walk.

START Roadside parking on Beulah road (B4358) near Newbridge-on-Wye, SO 016583.

PUBLIC TRANSPORT Newbridge-on-Wye is on bus routes to and from other towns in the area, including Llandrindod Wells.

All Saints,
Newbridge-on-Wye

13

LLANDEGLEY TO LLANDRINDOD WELLS

DESCRIPTION A walk of about 7½ miles from the village of Llandegley to Llandrindod Wells. This route climbs from the village to cross open access land with striking rock out-croppings and scenic views, before joining a lane, bridleway and footpath route to Llandrindod Wells. The latter part of the route passes a local viewpoint above Llandrindod Wells Lake. Allow about 4½ hours for the walk.

START Railway Station, car park and bus stops in central Llandrindod Wells, SO 059614.

PUBLIC TRANSPORT Powys bus ser-vice 46, Llandrindod Wells to Kington (for Hereford), passes along the main road adjacent to Llandegley village.

1 Alight from the bus on the main road, cross the road with care and head for St Tecla's church – part medieval, with a late medieval screen and ornate priest's door, the latter may have been brought from Abbey Cwmhir. The nave was rebuilt in 1876 and the tower in 1963. Cross the churchyard via kissing gates to the right of the church and descend a flight of steps. Cross the field to a gate and footbridge. Aim for the far left cor-ner of the next field, go through a gate and join a path leading uphill to a track. Turn LEFT on the track, continu-

2 Continue AHEAD to reach a stile just beyond a pond. Cross the stile and con-tinue AHEAD to the trig point. Follow the lower ground to the left of the trig point to reach a second stile. Cross and follow the higher ground on the left, then cross the ridge ahead between the two summits. On coming in sight of the lower ground on the left, head down towards this. Maintain direc-tion to join a bridleway leading to a way-marked gate.

3 Go through the gate and head HALF LEFT across open ground to reach a track. The bridleway marked on the map at this point appears to have been abandoned in favour of following the track around the field edges. (A County Council Rights of Way Officer has stated that this is the route used by most walkers and that an official diversion will be applied for in due course). Turn LEFT and follow the track through a gate. At the far corner of the next field, go through a gate on the right.

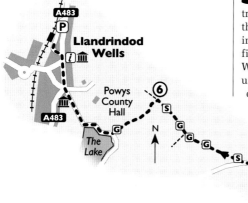

ing uphill. Go through a gate, passing a house on the right beyond trees. Continue AHEAD on the track, which now crosses open ground. Cross another track ascending from the right and continue uphill towards the high ground ahead.

Follow the track AHEAD and then round to the left. Go through a gate and follow the track AHEAD and then round to the right. Go through another two gates, by a rock outcropping on the right.

4 Bear HALF LEFT towards a group of conifers. Follow a path running just to the left of these, which soon becomes a track. Follow the track round to the right and then to the left. Follow the track along the brow of a hill and down to a junction with a lane. Turn LEFT on the lane. When the lane bends to the left (by conifers) turn RIGHT and go through a waymarked gate on the left. Bear RIGHT up the field towards two waymark posts. Continue AHEAD to a waymarked gate. Bear SLIGHTLY LEFT to a waymark post in mid-field, then bear towards the right hand (waymarked) gate further up the field. Continue past three waymark posts, passing to the left of a pond, to reach a waymarked gateway. Continue past a further two pairs of waymark posts. Follow the grassy track through two waymarked gateways.

5 Go through another five gates, pass a cottage on the right and continue downhill. When the track bends to the right, descend a small bank and follow a path just to the right of the fence. Cross a stile and turn RIGHT, heading down to a further stile. Follow the boundary on the right to a third stile. Cross and take the left hand footpath, which runs uphill and then bends round to the right to join a lane. Turn LEFT and follow the lane uphill, crossing the second stile on the right. Head up the bank to the trig point and cairns. From here follow a clear path AHEAD through three gates. Follow

a path that runs just to the left of a hawthorn tree. Skirt gorse bushes to reach a stile. Follow the path straight downhill, ignoring side turnings, to the edge of the wood.

6 On entering the wood, you are likely to notice a considerable number of paths – maintain a direction running roughly STRAIGHT AHEAD until reaching a large oak tree, with the beginnings of a cleft, on the right. Turn LEFT here and at the next junction of paths, bear RIGHT. After a few yards, turn RIGHT again on a path running down through a clearing to a waymark post. Turn LEFT and follow the path alongside the fence. At the next waymark post, take the right fork. Cross an open area and continue AHEAD on the path. Join

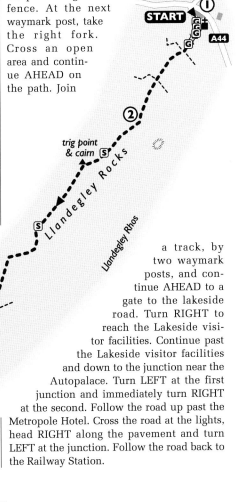

a track, by two waymark posts, and continue AHEAD to a gate to the lakeside road. Turn RIGHT to reach the Lakeside visitor facilities. Continue past the Lakeside visitor facilities and down to the junction near the Autopalace. Turn LEFT at the first junction and immediately turn RIGHT at the second. Follow the road up past the Metropole Hotel. Cross the road at the lights, head RIGHT along the pavement and turn LEFT at the junction. Follow the road back to the Railway Station.

LLANDRINDOD HILL

DESCRIPTION A 7 mile walk, climbing from Llandrindod Wells Lake, this route passes the old parish church and crosses upland pastures (and the local golf course) to the scenic hills and valleys to the east of Llandrindod Wells. Upland pastures and open access land with further excellent views are followed to reach Llanoley, from where the route returns to the lake via a local viewpoint. Allow about 4¼ hours for the walk.

START Llandrindod Wells Lake, SO 063606.

I From the Lakeside visitor facilities, follow the pavement around the Lake in a clockwise direction until reaching a picnic area sign on the right, near the lake lagoon. Cross the road with care and join the waymarked footpath opposite. Follow the path to the right of the fence and then head HALF RIGHT uphill, climbing a set of steps on route. On reaching a junction of paths, by an information board and two waymark posts, continue AHEAD for a few feet to a small gate. Pass through the gate and bear RIGHT towards the church. Bear HALF LEFT at the telegraph pole to reach a gate onto the road.

2 Cross the road to the next waymark post and follow the short track to the right of this. Go through a wooden gate into the churchyard - the church is originally 13th century but was rebuilt in 1894. Follow the short path ahead to a metal gate on the far side. Beyond the gate turn RIGHT, following the churchyard wall and then continuing to the corner of the field to pass through a small gate and descend a flight of steps. Turn LEFT on the track. Pass through a gate and make a sharp right hand turn onto the right hand track. Go through the next gateway and take the left fork in the track, alongside a fence on the left. When the fence turns uphill, continue AHEAD on a track that heads slightly to the left and climbs steadily between areas of bracken. Pass through a gate and continue AHEAD along the track, passing between

sheep feeders. At the next waymark post (on the left near a field gate) turn HALF LEFT and go uphill to another stile in the fence ahead.

3 Cross the long field to another stile just to the right of a gate. Just after crossing the stile, turn LEFT and follow a path up through bracken to a waymarked stile in the top left hand corner of the field. Cross and continue up the hill to a waymarked gate in the top right hand corner, onto the golf course. Keep close to the fence on the right and follow the footpath around the edge of the golf course (keep an eye out for golf balls!). Ignore stiles without waymarking (these appear to give golfers access to adjacent fields). Eventually, cross a waymarked stile on the right and head diagonally across the field to reach a gate, next to a stone wall. Pass through and follow the wall along the right hand side of the field to the second (waymarked) gate. Pass through and head across the field, aiming to the left of a line of trees to reach a stile (part hidden by the trees). Cross and continue HALF LEFT to reach a stile onto a lane.

4 Turn LEFT in the lane and continue to a t-junction. Turn RIGHT and follow the lane down, through a bend to the left. Take the right fork at the base of the hill and very soon take another right fork in the track, passing between a house and a lake. Take

16

the right fork at another waymark sign and follow the track over two cattlegrids. At the next fork in the track, bear LEFT. Go through a gate and after a few yards take the right fork. Continue to follow the track, which soon has a fence running to its left. On reaching a left hand corner in the fence, turn LEFT and follow the track through a gate. Continue up the

Map labels: Upper Llanoley, Lower Llanoley, (7), Bank House, Pen-rhiw Frank, Carreg-wiber Bank, Bwlchyfedwen, N, Carregwiber, (4), cairn, Gilwern Hill, (5), (6), 0 Miles ½

track, which now becomes grassy – the remains of an old fence can be seen on the right for part of this stretch. Maintain direction until reaching the junction with a wider stony track running parallel to a fenceline.

5 Turn LEFT on the wider track and follow this uphill and round to the left (ignore the bridleway sign on the right). Before coming to a gate across the main track, turn RIGHT and go through a small waymarked gate at the top of a short bank. Continue AHEAD up the rise and cross over a track. Continue in the same direction, aiming to the right of a cairn on a small hill to the left. On sighting a small gate in the fence ahead, make for this. Go through and continue AHEAD to a second small gate a few yards to the left of a larger gate. Go through the small gate and continue to follow the grassy track ahead. On nearing the hill on the right, bear HALF RIGHT and climb the hill, keeping roughly parallel to the fence on the right. Go through

a gate in the right hand corner of the field to reach a cairn.

6 When ready continue down the hill, heading HALF LEFT. At base of the hill, head LEFT on a fairly faint track running to the left of a fence. Go through a gate on the right, fording a small stream. Follow the left hand side of the field, to recross the stream and go through a gate. Continue to follow the track AHEAD, in due course passing a cottage (Pen-rhiw Frank) on the right. Follow the track down to Llanoley, bearing RIGHT on the bridleway rather than following a footpath on the left. Pass through a gate and continue along the track to join the end of a lane.

7 Climb the hill, passing Lower and Upper Llanoley on the right. Take the second stile on the right. Head up the bank to the trig point and cairns. From here, follow a clear path AHEAD through three waymarked gates. Follow a path that runs just to the left of a hawthorn tree. Skirt gorse bushes to reach a stile. Follow the path running straight downhill, ignoring side turnings, to reach the edge of the wood.

8 On entering the woodland, you are likely to notice a considerable number of paths – maintain a direction running roughly STRAIGHT AHEAD until reaching a large oak tree, with the beginnings of a cleft, on the right. Turn LEFT here and at the next junction of paths, bear RIGHT. After a few yards, turn RIGHT again on a path running down through a clearing to a waymark post. Turn LEFT and follow the path alongside the field boundary. At the next waymark post, take the right fork. Cross an open area and continue AHEAD on the path. Join a track, by two waymark posts, and continue AHEAD to reach a gate onto the lakeside road. Turn RIGHT to return to the Lakeside visitor facilities.

LLANDRINDOD WELLS TO BUILTH WELLS

DESCRIPTION A 10 mile walk, interesting not only for its views but for the variety of scenery that it includes – lakeside, woodland, upland sheep pastures, fields, country lanes, open hill and finally a stretch alongside the River Wye. Allow about 6 hours for the walk. Note that the permissive cycle route at the end of this walk is not available to walkers during Royal Welsh Agricultural Show Week in July.

START Llandrindod Wells Lake, SO 063606

PUBLIC TRANSPORT Several Powys bus services, including numbers 47 and 704 connect Llandrindod Wells and Builth Wells, passing through Howey on route.

I Starting From the Lakeside visitor facilities, follow the pavement around the Lake in a clockwise direction until reaching a picnic area sign on the right, near the lake lagoon. Cross the road with care and join the waymarked footpath opposite. Follow the path to the right of the fence and then head HALF RIGHT uphill, climbing a set of steps on route. On reaching a junction of paths, by an information board and two waymark posts, continue AHEAD for a few feet to a small gate. Pass through the gate and bear RIGHT towards the church. Bear HALF LEFT at the telegraph pole to reach a gate onto the road. Cross the road to the next waymark post and follow the short track to the right of this. Go through a wooden gate into the churchyard – *the church is originally 13th century but was rebuilt in 1894.* Follow the short path ahead to a metal gate on the far side. Beyond the gate turn RIGHT, following the churchyard wall and then continuing to the corner of the field to pass through a small gate and descend a flight of steps to a track.

2 Turn LEFT on the track. Pass through a gate and make a SHARP RIGHT HAND TURN onto the right hand track. Go through the next gateway and take the left fork in the track,

alongside a fence on the left. When the fence turns uphill, continue AHEAD on a track that heads slightly to the left and climbs steadily between areas of bracken. Pass through a gate and continue along the track, passing between sheep feeders. At the next waymark post (on the left near a field gate) turn HALF LEFT and go uphill to another stile in the fence ahead. Cross the long field to another stile just to the right of a gate. Follow the path AHEAD through bracken. At the next waymark post, follow the path STRAIGHT AHEAD to reach a waymarked gate on the right. Go through and follow the path AHEAD to the next waymark post (amongst bracken to the left). Turn RIGHT here and follow a path that runs downhill, parallel to a fence on the left. On reaching a clear area at the base of the bank, turn LEFT. Follow the path to the left of the fence, passing a waymark post on the corner. Follow the path to a stile in the fence. Cross and head RIGHT on a track leading to a gate into a lane.

3 Turn RIGHT in the lane and head downhill and round a bend to the left. (This lane gives access to and from the Llandrindod Wells-Builth Wells bus route, on the main road adjacent to Howey village). When the lane bends to the right, turn LEFT into the waymarked driveway leading to Acorn Court and Three Wells B&Bs. Shortly after passing the turning for Acorn Court, cross the stile on the right. Go straight across the field to a footbridge and stile. Head HALF LEFT across the next field to another stile, then cut across the corner of a third field to reach a footbridge and stile to the right. Cross the fourth field, passing under telegraph wires on route, to reach a stile to right of a gate. Follow the track along the left hand side of the field. Go STRAIGHT AHEAD through two gates in quick succession and continue along the track. Take the left fork at a junction of tracks and go through another gate into a wooded area. Continue along the track to a stile in the fence on the right. Cross and head HALF LEFT up the bank, passing just to the left of an old farm building. Continue AHEAD on a grassy track that leads to the junction with an access track. Turn LEFT on the access track and walk up to the junction with a road. (This road also provides access to and from the Llandrindod Wells-Builth Wells bus route).

Llandrindod Wells | **START**

4 Turn LEFT on the road (which follows the course of an old Drover's Route to Kington in England) and follow this for about three-quarters of a mile, passing a side road and a driveway to the right. Take the third turning to the right, by a Post Box. Follow the scenic lane for about one mile, until the lane bends to the right. Go straight AHEAD through a waymarked gate and follow the track, passing a ruined cottage (Tynlliddiart) on the left, to reach a second gate giving access onto the Carneddau hills. On reaching the open land, turn LEFT and ascend the hill until above the bracken line. Bear RIGHT at this point and follow the high ground towards the south (there are good views on this stretch). Look for and head towards a fence and old wall to the right. Follow the path running to the left of this boundary. The path runs roughly parallel to the fence for some way and then skirts around the shoulders of the hills at the southern end of the Carneddau. *The two southernmost hills are the sites of two hill forts – Caer Fawr being near the walking route (the northern banks and ditches of this can be seen from the walking route) and Caer Einon off to the left.* After about two miles, cross a small stream and take the broader track that bends slightly to the left. Continue on this track, now passing above farmland on the left. Pass through a gate and continue AHEAD on the track, which is now waymarked, passing through a further three gates. Pass above Maengowan Farm and turn RIGHT onto the farm access track.

5 Descend, passing through a gate across the access track. Continue to descend the main track until reaching a bridleway waymark sign on the left. Turn LEFT onto the bridleway and descend to reach another junction with the main access track. At this point, either of the fol-

The Lake

Broomy Hill

Three Wells

Howey

Crossway

N

A483

0 — Miles — 1

Caer fawr

Llanelwedd Rocks

woodland alternative

River Wye

Builth Wells

lowing two routes can be used:

● RIVERSIDE ROUTE
Turn LEFT and follow the access track until reaching the junction with the A481. Cross the main road junction with care and take the side road into the Wyeside Trading Estate opposite. Follow the road round to the left, continuing AHEAD on a road marked as 'Permissive Cycle Route'. Follow this round a bend to the right and shortly thereafter take a tarmac path leading off to the left. This follows the route of the Brecon to Llanidloes Railway, 1864-1963. Continue on the waymarked cycle route which follows the River Wye by a mixture of tarmac path and lane to join the road near Builth Wells. On reaching the road, turn LEFT to cross the bridge into town. Take the first turn on the right to reach the bus stops near the Black Bull statue.

● WOODLAND ROUTE
Cross the access track and follow the next (woodland) section of the waymarked bridleway to the junction with the A483. Turn LEFT and follow the verge for a short way to the junction with the A481. Cross with care and turn RIGHT on the pavement. Follow this past the church and school. Look out for a kissing gate on the left. Go through this and cross a short stretch of open ground to a tarmac path. Turn RIGHT and follow the path to join the road near Builth Wells. On reaching the road, turn LEFT to cross the bridge into town. Take the first turn on the right to reach the bus stops near the Black Bull statue.

The Bower

The Banks

410m ▲

Carneddau

▲
432m

LLANDRINDOD WELLS TO NEWBRIDGE-ON-WYE

DESCRIPTION A 5½ mile walk, mostly along footpaths and quiet lanes. This route provides views of countryside and surrounding hills, as well as the opportunity to visit a local wetland nature reserve. There is a bus access point about half way through the walk as well as in Newbridge-on-Wye. There is the option of a pub lunch in Newbridge. Allow up to 3 hours.
START Llandrindod Wells Lake.
SO 063606.
PUBLIC TRANSPORT Llandrindod Wells is on the Heart of Wales Railway Line and has several bus services, including the TrawsCambria Brecon-Newtown. Newbridge-on-Wye is on the bus route to and from Llandrindod Wells, as well as other local towns.

I Starting from the Lakeside visitor facilities, follow the pavement around the lake in a clockwise direction until reaching the picnic area on the right. Cross the road with care and join the waymarked footpath opposite. Follow the path, which is at first gravelled, up through trees to reach the junction with another path. Cross the second path and exit the woodland via a footgate. Turn RIGHT and follow the path towards the old parish church visible ahead. Go through a gate and cross the road to reach the old parish church – *originally 13th Century, rebuilt in 1894*. Go through a wooden gate to the left side of the church grounds and cross to the footgate opposite.

2 Turn RIGHT and follow the line of the wall around the church grounds till reaching the corner of the field. Pass through a gate and descend a flight of steps to a track. Turn RIGHT and follow the track for a short way. On reaching a waymark post on the right, bear LEFT up the bank towards a way-marked stile. Cross and bear HALF RIGHT, following the line of the trees and passing to the left of a house to reach another track. Turn LEFT on the track.

3 Continue AHEAD on the track (the entrance to Pentrosfa Mire Nature Reserve is on the right – *the reserve can be visited via a stile from this section of the walk* – after which return to the main route and turn RIGHT). Continue AHEAD through a waymarked gate and follow the left hand boundary of the next two fields. Towards the end of the second field, bear HALF RIGHT to reach a stile.

4 Cross and continue HALF RIGHT across the next field. Turn RIGHT to walk between hedges for a short way, then cross a stile on the left. Continue along the right hand side of the next field to a further stile. Cross and continue for a short way to a stile on the right. Cross and head for the far left corner of the next field. Cross a stile into a clump of trees. Pass through these and continue HALF LEFT on a clear path – *passing*

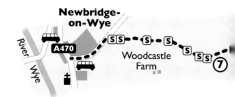

Caer Du earthworks on the left – to reach a kissing gate onto an enclosed track.

5 Follow the track to the junction with a minor road. Turn RIGHT and then LEFT and follow the road through Howey village. (The mid-walk bus access point can be reached by turning RIGHT just after the village shop – buses to Builth Wells stop just to the right of the junction. For buses to Llandrindod, use the lay-by opposite). After passing the village shop, continue AHEAD between the Telephone Box and the Village Hall. At the end of this road, follow the path down to the pavement and head LEFT along the main road to the staggered crossroads. Cross the road with care and take the right turn, signposted for Newbridge-on-Wye and Disserth. Follow this quiet road for about one mile to reach Disserth – *there are good views of the church on the way down.*

6 Cross the bridge – *good views of the Ithon at this point* – then turn LEFT onto a footpath. Follow the left boundary of the field over a footbridge, into another section of woodland. Climb the wooden steps up the bank (this is steep but not very long) and continue through the woodland to a stile. Cross the field beyond, then cross a track by means of stiles. Turn RIGHT, keeping close the fence on the right. On reaching a waymark arrow, on the remains of a tree, head along the right hand side of the field (passing another waymark arrow on the remains of a tree stump to the right of a gate).

7 Cross a stile to the right of a gate and continue along the right hand side of the next field, Cross a stile and then turn RIGHT to cross a second stile. Aim slightly to the left when crossing the next two fields, connected by stiles, passing through a line of trees between these. Head along the left side of the next field to a stile. Follow the path along the old boundary of the field to reach a stile just to the left of a telegraph pole, then cross the final field to a stile giving onto a road. Turn LEFT and follow the pavement into Newbridge-on-Wye.

LLANDRINDOD WELLS' GREEN SPACES

DESCRIPTION An attractive walk of about 4 miles, via Temple Gardens, Memorial Gardens and County Hall grounds to the Lake and the adjacent Woodland Walk. The route then leads across a grassy area and by quiet road and lane to a footpath leading to Rock Park where an attractive riverside walk is followed above the Ithon. The latter stages of the Rock Park section go past an attractive area of wetland and bog garden. The route also passes a considerable number of information boards, including some about the local heritage. (This route can be muddy in places.) Allow about 2½ hours for the walk.

START Bus stops, car park and railway station in central Llandrindod Wells, SO 059614.

I From the railway station (booking office side of the line) head RIGHT past Boots and turn RIGHT into Middleton Street. Cross the junction at the end of Middleton Street to Temple Gardens (see the Information Boards near the entrance to the gardens). Bear LEFT through the gardens, passing to the left of the Bandstand and heading towards the Metropole Hotel (see additional information boards towards the far side of the gardens). On reaching the road, turn LEFT, head for and use the pedestrian crossing, then turn RIGHT to reach Memorial Gardens (where there is a further information board). Go through the gardens, passing the entrance to the local Tourist Information Centre and also the local Museum (well worth a visit). When ready, continue through Memorial Gardens, crossing a footbridge on route. Turn RIGHT at the road and follow this past the town library (on the left). On reaching the t-junction, cross and follow the driveway half left up towards County Hall. Ignore the first footpath sign on the right, go past the statue of Gaea on the right and take the footpath on the right. Follow this STRAIGHT AHEAD to

the next road, passing through an old gate on route, and turn LEFT at the road. *This section of the route passes trees planted in 1946 to commemorate Brecon and Radnor's contribution to the Red Cross Agriculture Fund. The remains of St Maelog's Chapel – built in the late 12th century and demolished in the 16th – can be seen on the left.* Continue *around the Lake – created in 1872-3 on the site of a former peat bog - keeping to the left hand side of the road and passing a picnic area and ornate metal gates on the left. (The carving to the left of the gates is one of the characters from the 'Llandoddies' book – see stage 3 below).*

2 Follow the pavement to the end, near a 'Llandrindod Lake Park Woodland' information board. Go through the gate on the left and follow the track ahead, very soon taking the right fork. When the track bends to the left, by two waymark posts, take the path running ahead. After crossing a more open grassy area, turn RIGHT here, cross a very small stream and turn SHARP RIGHT on a path through the woods – there is a small waymark post nearby. Pass through a kissing gate and continue AHEAD to reach a junction of paths, with another information board visible off to the right. Continue AHEAD at this point, now on a gravelled path that bears half left and then descends to the road. On reaching the road, turn LEFT and follow the lakeside pavement around the Lake to reach the Craft Shop, restaurant and other facilities.

3 Standing outside the Lakeside Craft Shop, facing the Lake, turn RIGHT and go to the end of the building. See the information board on the end wall of the building, about 'Llandoddies' and then head up the short tarmac slope and head LEFT to the 'Llandoddie' carving. Take the path leading up the bank from near this figure, onto the Common. Go STRAIGHT AHEAD across the grass and follow a gravelled path through the trees. Turn LEFT and cross another area of grass to pass through a line of commemorative trees – *planted to mark the coronation of George VI in 1936* – and head RIGHT down to the Ridgebourne shops. Go over the pedes-

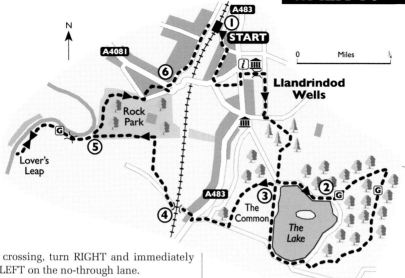

trian crossing, turn RIGHT and immediately turn LEFT on the no-through lane.

4 Pass under the Heart of Wales Railway Bridge and shortly thereafter bear HALF RIGHT on a waymarked footpath. Follow the path to the right of wooden fencing and continue AHEAD to reach the entrance to Rock Park – *the open area to the right is the site of a Roman practice ground*. On reaching the trees at the edge of the park, turn LEFT on a tarmac path and follow this downhill to a service road. Turn LEFT on this, passing the Bowling Club (on the right). Continue AHEAD and, at the next junction, continue AHEAD following the waymark sign. Ignore the next waymark post and continue AHEAD, descending to a footbridge and kissing gate. Follow the Ithon along the edge of the field (the stepping-stones shown on the map are no longer present). At the end of the field, retrace your steps to and through the kissing gate and over the footbridge.

5 After a few feet, leave the main track and bear HALF LEFT up the bank to metal railings. Follow the railings uphill, passing a circular seat and an information board about the birdlife that can be seen in Rock Park. Shortly afterwards, turn LEFT down a flight of waymarked steps and follow a path above the River Ithon. Follow the path past the first waymark sign and turn LEFT at a waymark sign alongside a t-junction of paths. Follow the path above a stream on the left. At the next waymark post bear HALF LEFT towards an ornamental wooden 'well'. Go a short distance past this to reach the Rock Park Visitor Centre. Head LEFT around the building and cross the car park area. Continue AHEAD, following the waymark sign that leads down past wooden railings on the left, to the Chalybeate Spring. Continue to head LEFT and, at a junction of paths, take the second path from the right. Very soon, turn LEFT onto a gravel path that bears right, leading uphill through the newly established 'bog garden' area. Rejoin the main path near the exit from Rock Park and head LEFT to the road junction.

6 Cross the road on the left, passing the front of Y Gwalia – the former Radnorshire Council Headquarters. Cross the next road and continue AHEAD along the High Street – *some of the buildings on the left have recently been renovated, as part of the High Street Improvement Project* – to reach a 19th century red brick building (currently the Magistrate's Court and Police Station) opposite the railway station. The road on the left, immediately after the red brick building, leads to the Llanerch Inn, an 18th century coaching inn.

WALK 14
LLANDRINDOD WELLS TO CROSSGATES

DESCRIPTION A linear walk of about 5 miles (if returning by bus) or 6¼ miles (if returning by train). This route visits a small nature reserve, and then heads up through deciduous woodland to a hilltop walk with excellent views before descending by footpath and track to the scenic Ithon valley. From here, footpaths, tracks and lanes are followed through fields, including riverside sections, to reach Crossgates (where bus and train services are available to return to Llandrindod Wells). Allow about 3 or 3¾ hours for the walk.

START Tourist Information Centre, Memorial Gardens, SO 061613.

PUBLIC TRANSPORT Powys Buses 46, 47 and 704 link Crossgates with Llandrindod Wells. The Heart of Wales Railway Line has a request stop near Crossgates for Llandrindod Wells.

I From outside the Tourist Information Centre, head LEFT past the Museum and over the footbridge. At the road, turn LEFT. At the crossroads, turn RIGHT into Broadway and follow this up the T-junction at the far end. Turn LEFT and follow the road past the turnings for 'Woodlands' and 'Hillside Lane'. At the end of the uphill section (before the housing estate and the Post Box on the right) turn RIGHT through a foot-entrance next to a metal gate. Follow the tarmac path along the right-hand-side of Gorse Farm Nature Reserve – look out for an information board on the left. Cross the footbridge and ascend the steps, then bear LEFT to reach a second Radnorshire Wildlife Information Board. When ready, return to the path and turn LEFT to go between houses to a road.

2 Bear LEFT, RIGHT and LEFT again to reach a T-junction. Turn RIGHT at the T-junction and follow the road for a few yards to a waymark sign on the left. Follow the footpath on the left between fences to reach a gate into a field. Head HALF LEFT across the

field, passing to the right of a rock and continue AHEAD, up through a wooded dingle, above a stream on the right. Pass through a gate and follow a short path up through gorse bushes. Continue HALF RIGHT up the field and cross a stile into a forestry plantation. After a short distance, bear LEFT on a path that cuts diagonally through the small plantation to a stile.

3 Cross the stile and head HALF RIGHT to reach a track. Turn LEFT on the track and follow this past a permissive path waymark post, on the left. Follow the track around the left hand side of the hill and begin to descend. On reaching a stile on the left there are two options – EITHER cross the stile and head down the field to a second stile to the left of a gate OR continue to follow the permissive route down the track, through a gate and to the road. On reaching the road, turn RIGHT and follow the road past Bailey Einon Farm on the left. At a T-junction, turn RIGHT and start down the hill, looking out for a waymarked stile on the left.

4 Cross the stile and head down the left hand side of the field to a stile in the far left corner. Cross and turn RIGHT to go through a gate. Turn LEFT and go through a second gate. Cross the bridge over the River Ithon and follow the path AHEAD, soon between two rows of trees. Beyond the end of the trees, bear RIGHT and go through a gate. Turn LEFT on the track and follow this along the base of the hill. On nearing Neuadd, cross a stile just to the left of a gate. Follow the track along the right hand side of the first field and half right across the second field to reach a further stile. Turn LEFT on the lane and follow this past Neuadd Isaf.

5 At the road junction, turn LEFT. Follow the lane for about ¾ mile to the bend near 'Alpine View' (on the left). Turn LEFT just before the house, going through the left hand of two gates. Continue AHEAD for a few yards, then bear HALF LEFT, following way-mark posts along the field. Towards the far side of the field, bear HALF RIGHT on a path leading to Alpine Bridge. Cross and follow the path on the other side, up to a gate onto a track. Turn RIGHT on the track and follow this through a gate. Follow the track along the left hand side of the field to a further gate. Pass through and continue along the right hand side of the next field.

6 When the track turns left, continue AHEAD to pass through a further gateway by an old stile. Immediately beyond the gateway, turn RIGHT and follow the right hand edge of the fields to the River Ithon. Turn LEFT and follow the river bank along to a stile to the right of a gate. Head up a track, which is joined by another track from the left. Look out for a waymark post on a bank to the right. Turn RIGHT at the waymark post and head down the right hand side of the field to a stile. Cross and continue AHEAD, descending to the right of a farm building.

7 Cross a stile and continue HALF LEFT along the field to a further stile. Follow the path up wooden steps and cross a stile onto the roadside. Turn RIGHT and cross the Ithon Bridge. TO REACH THE BUS STOP, continue along the main road until reaching the bus shelter (on the right). TO REACH THE RAILWAY STATION, continue along the main road for a short way, passing a lay-by,

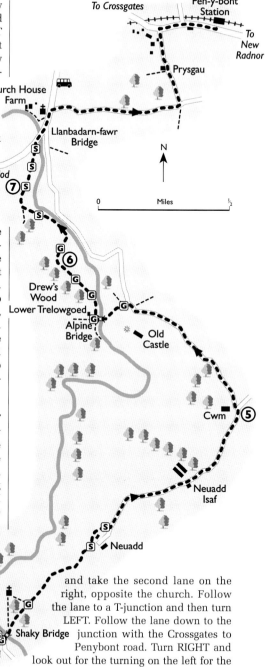

and take the second lane on the right, opposite the church. Follow the lane to a T-junction and then turn LEFT. Follow the lane down to the junction with the Crossgates to Penybont road. Turn RIGHT and look out for the turning on the left for the station (Penybont is a request stop, so signal as for a bus).

1 Go through a kissing gate to the right of the car park and head for a stile on

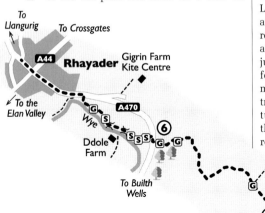

To Llangurig
To Crossgates
Rhayader Gigrin Farm Kite Centre
A44
To the Elan Valley
A470
Wye
Ddole Farm
⑥ G S S S G G G
To Builth Wells
G
⑤ G
Druid's Circle G
▲477 m
Carn Wen G
G
◆④
Pen-y-ffynnon
G Nant-glas
Bry can

passes between areas of bracken. Descend to a stile. Continue down the grassy track, with Llyn Gwyn soon coming into view. Cross a grassy area and continue downhill until reaching a stile into the forestry area. Cross and follow the path downhill to reach the junction with a forestry track. Turn left and follow the rough section for a few yards/metres to a turning area. Continue along the track, gradually descending to reach a sharp turn to the right near a small waterfall on the left. Continue down the main track until reaching a gate out of the forestry area.

the far side of the play area. Follow the left hand side of the field, passing through a gap in the old fence. Cross two stiles and then cross a third stile to the right of a house. Head across the field to reach a stile onto a lane. Turn LEFT and follow the lane to the end. Go through the gate ahead and follow the track along the left hand side of the field. Follow the track to a further two gates. Continue to follow the track to the point where this bends to the right, then head up the bank to a stile. Cross and go up the left hand side of the field to a further stile. Head up to the top left hand corner of the next field and then turn RIGHT. Go along the top of the field to reach a stile on the left. Cross and head along the left hand side of the next two fields, connected by a stile. Continue along the left hand side of a third field to reach a stile and footbridge. Cross and head along the right hand side of the field to a four-way waymark post. Cross the stile and head HALF LEFT to reach a track. Turn LEFT and follow the track through a gate.

2 Continue along the track until just beyond the trees to the right then bear half right up the field to a stile. Cross and bear half left to a further stile. Bear right up the hill, aiming to the right of the TV Mast. Cross the ridge at the lowest point, to the right of the mast. Continue ahead on a grassy track that

3 Go through the gate and turn left on the track. Cross a bridge and go up a slight rise. Soon after this, look out for metal gates on either side of the track. Go through the gate on the right and follow a path across the field to a gate into the area around the lake. When ready, retrace the route across the field and turn right. Follow the track to the junction with a lane. Turn LEFT and follow the lane to and through Nant-glas village, taking the right fork at the junction by the phone box. Look for a no-through lane leading right, next to a forestry plantation (a Caerhyddwen Forest sign can be seen amongst the trees). Turn RIGHT onto the lane and follow it through a gate and to the point where it bends left towards Pen-y-ffynnon.

4 At this point, turn RIGHT on an access track and, after a few feet, go through the small waymarked gate on the left. Head up the right hand side of the field to a gate. Turn RIGHT and follow the path along the edge of the open access land. Soon take the left hand, slightly higher, path. Go through a gate and continue AHEAD on the path to reach a further gate. Continue AHEAD across the open ground towards a waymark post just to the right of a gate. Although not on a right of way, several cairns etc can be seen off to the left during this section of the walk. Go through the gate and follow the bridleway route going STRAIGHT AHEAD.

5 Go past two ridges of outcroppings and continue AHEAD for a striking view of Rhayader and the hills surrounding the town. Descend the hill, on a track that leads down to the left and then makes a sharp right hand turn. Go through a gate and continue along the track, AHEAD and then round to the RIGHT. Continue downhill, following a number of yellow-topped waymark posts (these indicate the route of Gigrin Farm Trail as well as the bridleway). On reaching a fence, go through the first of two gates and follow the path to the left of the fence (now within RSPB woodland). Follow the path downhill, going RIGHT at the fork, to reach a gate onto the road.

6 Head RIGHT along the verge for a few yards and then cross the road with care, heading for a stile on the far side. Cross and head down the left hand side of the field. Cross another stile and follow the waymarked path around the boundary of the fence. Cross a stile and footbridge and follow riverside route to a further footbridge and stile. Continue along the riverside, passing a

WALK 15

LLANYRE TO RHAYADER

DESCRIPTION Starting from the village of Llanyre* near Llandrindod Wells, this 8¾ mile route climbs up to a ridge with views back towards Llandrindod Wells and ahead towards Rhayader. From the ridge there is also a view of Llyn Gwyn, once a fishing lake owned by Abbey Cwmhir. Descending through forestry, there is a short detour to visit Llyn Gwyn, before the walk continues through the village of Nant-glas** to join a bridleway leading over a hill to the Wye Valley. The route down to the river leads through the edge of an RSPB Nature Reserve, before joining a riverside path into Rhayader. Allow about 5¼ hours for the walk.

*Llanyre is on the bus route between Llandrindod Wells and Rhayader. The village can also be reached by following the cycling/walking route in 'Castell Collen, Llanfihangel Helygen and Llanyre'.

** This walk can be divided into two using the 47 bus, which passes along the A470, about 1 mile west of Nant-glas.

START Car park across the lane from The Bell Country Inn, SO 044624.

PUBLIC TRANSPORT Llanyre is on Powys Bus Route 47, travelling between Llandrindod Wells and Rhayader.

pipeline across the river. Go through a gate at the far end of the field and follow the path AHEAD and then round to the right to reach the road. Turn LEFT and follow the road into Rhayader, going straight over the crossroads by the Town Clock. The bus shelter is in the car park on the right just beyond the Leisure Centre.

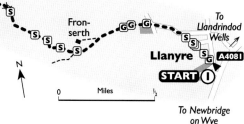

WALK 16

PENYBONT COMMON

DESCRIPTION Walks of either 4 or 8 miles. The longer route includes an attractive walk along a quiet lane with hedges and excellent views to the north. Penybont Village attractions include The Old Thomas Shop (shop, museum, cafe and gallery) and the **Severn Arms** (pub lunch and beer garden). Penybont Common was also the scene of a Quaker Revival in the 19th century. The Common (rough grazing with some patches of low-growing gorse) is open access land that gives a range of good views of the hills around. Allow about 2 or 4 hours for the walks, plus time to visit the village attractions.

START Either Penybont Railway Station. SO 099649) or Penybont Village. SO 116642.

PUBLIC TRANSPORT Penybont Railway Station (Heart of Wales Line – local information 01597 822053).

I **If starting from Penybont Station** (*8 mile option*), turn RIGHT on leaving the station. Take the first turning on the left and turn LEFT again at the T-junction. Follow the quiet lane (attractive hedges and views to the north) for about two miles to Penybont Village. At the junction with the main road, turn RIGHT and head down into the village.

The starting point for walkers joining the route in Penybont Village (*4 mile option*) – places to visit on the main road include the bridge over the River Ithon, The Old Thomas Shop and the **Severn Arms Hotel** (pub lunch available). To access the Common, take the Knighton road. Turn LEFT onto a waymarked footpath, crossing a stile on the left, just before a cattle grid.

2 The Common is now open access land but the following route gives good views of the land around. Follow the left hand boundary of the Common, which provides hill views and is bounded by attractive trees in places. At the further end of the Common, head back alongside the road and eventually cross to the southern half of the Common and bear HALF RIGHT. Keep to the higher ground on the way back towards the south. On approaching the main road, turn RIGHT onto a track that skirts a line of trees and return to Penybont Village.

3 To return to Penybont Station, follow the main road out of the village, passing the wooded grounds of the Hall (on the left) and turn LEFT onto the lane followed on the outward route. At the junction, turn RIGHT and head down towards the main road. Turn RIGHT again and follow the main road to the turning for the station, on the left. Penybont is a request stop, so signal as for a bus.

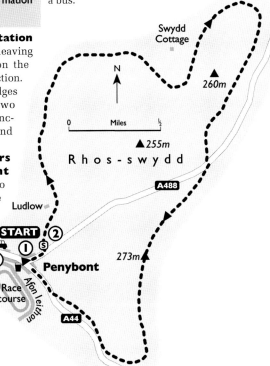

28

1 From the road junction near the church, follow the Wye Valley Walk along a no-through lane passing to the left of the church. Follow the lane, which includes riverside sections, until reaching the entrance track to Careg-yn-fol, on the left. Bear HALF RIGHT here, following the Wye Valley Walk through a gate onto a track that now runs through National Trust land.

2 Ignore the first waymarked route leading off to the right. Continue AHEAD on the track, looking out for a gap in the trees on the left that allows a view across the valley to Doldowlod House (once owned by James Watt and still the property of his descendants). After passing this point, look out for a second waymarked route leading off to the right.

WALK 17

TREMBYDD CIRCULAR

DESCRIPTION A 5¼ mile walk from Llanwrthwl that initially uses the Wye Valley Walk, along a lane and then a track. A bridleway then leads uphill (allowing views across the valley that include the Wye, the course of a former railway line and Doldowlod House, which was once owned by the inventor James Watt). After a circuit of Trembyd hill, the route follows a footpath and bridleway back to the Wye Valley Walk to return to Llanwrthwl. Allow about 3 hours for the walk.

START Llanwrthwl, SO 976637.

PUBLIC TRANSPORT Powys Bus 47 stops on the main road at the entrance to Llanwrthwl, connecting the village to Rhayader, Builth Wells and Llandrindod Wells.

4 Head HALF RIGHT up to the top of Trembyd for views of the hills around. Continue along the Trembyd ridge and, when sighting the lower-lying area in Rhos Cilgolgwm, strike off to the right to join the zigzag route of Rhiw Llanwrthwl as this track descends the hill. At the base of the hill, turn RIGHT and follow the path along the base of the hill until reaching the course of the Wye Valley Walk. Turn LEFT and follow the track and lane back to Llanwrthwl.

3 Follow the second bridleway uphill (look back about half way up for an excellent view across the Wye Valley, with river, course of old railway line and Doldowlod House all visible). Follow the track round to the right. Ignore a path coming up from the left and continue to ascend the open access land. On reaching a waymarked gate into a field, do not go through this but turn RIGHT and follow the field boundary to the corner of the fence.

Llanwrthwl

① START

A470

River Wye

Hodrid

G ②

③

Wye Valley Walk

④

N

Trembyd 475 m

0 — Miles — ½

TWO BRIDGES
& GREEN LANES

DESCRIPTION An 8 mile walk. Starting from the (Victorian) man-made Llandrindod Lake, this route climbs through woodland and hill pastures to a viewpoint, before descending to Cefnllys, the site of a medieval town of which only the church now remains. The riverside location is overlooked by a hill that was the site of a Marcher Castle. Nearby is Bailey Einon Nature Reserve, from which the walk runs through woods and fields to Alpine Bridge, where the Ithon cuts through a small gorge. The return journey to the Lake follows a mixture of woodland and hill paths, providing further good views of the area. Allow about 4¾ hours for the walk

START Llandrindod Wells Lake, SO 063606.

I From the Lakeside visitor facilities, cross the lakeside road and turn RIGHT. Follow the pavement to the end, near a 'Llandrindod Lake Park Woodland' information board. Go through the gate on the left and follow the track ahead, soon taking the right fork. When the track bends to the left, by two waymark posts, take the path ahead. After crossing an open grassy area, look for a two-way waymark post, near the fence ahead. Take the left fork and follow the path alongside the fence to a waymark post near a stile. Do not cross the stile, but turn RIGHT and follow the path up the bank. At a junction of paths, turn LEFT and soon take the left fork. On reaching a large oak tree, turn RIGHT and follow the path uphill and out of the woods. Continue uphill towards a patch of gorse. Cross a stile and skirt the gorse, then continue uphill towards the next fence. Continue AHEAD on a path that leads through three waymarked gates, up to the trig point.

2 Continue AHEAD to a stile onto the lane and turn LEFT. Head down the lane, ignoring the permissive route on the left. Continue down the lane until reaching the track for Upper Llanoley (there is a waymark sign on the fence to the right of the entrance and a waymark post on the other side of the

lane). Turn LEFT here and follow the track, passing the turning for the house, to reach a waymarked gate. Continue along the track, descending towards Cefnllys – look for two gates on the left leading into an area of 'permissive open access' wood. Pass through a gate across the track and follow the track round to the left. Pass through a second gate onto a lane, follow this to the RIGHT until reaching the entrance gates into Bailey Einon Nature Reserve and the area around St Michael's Church.

3 Turn LEFT into Bailey Einon Nature Reserve. Follow the path through the reserve, taking either route on reaching a fork in the boardwalk (these rejoin later on). Continue along the boardwalk and pass through a gate at the far end – there are handrails at the steeper sections of the path from this point. Continue along a more level section of the path with a fence to the right. Climb alongside railings for a short way, then descend back to level ground – from this point look for a clear path leading half left up to a stile. Cross and continue up the bank to a waymark post. Head RIGHT along the field and cross a stile. Follow the right hand boundary of the field to another stile. Take the right hand footpath along the right hand side of the field and then down to a stile a little way to the left of a house.

4 Cross stile, track and stile on far side. Continue AHEAD to a stile and shallow stream. Head across the right hand corner of the next field to the next stile. Head towards a stile just to the left of a large oak near a wood. Cross the stile and take a path (faint for the first few yards) that runs to the left for a short way and then turns half right up the bank. At the top of the wood, exit via a gate on the left and proceed up the bank to a waymark post. Turn RIGHT and continue AHEAD past a two-way marker post and through a gate. Continue AHEAD, in line with the farm buildings on the other side of the river. On reaching the riverbank, by a waymark post, turn LEFT and follow the track through a gate and a wood. Go up the field to a gate onto a farm track. Head RIGHT on the track for a few feet to a gate on the right, leading to Alpine Bridge.

5 When ready, go back to the farm track. Turn LEFT on this and follow it round to the right, past the farm buildings. Go through a gate and follow the track along the right hand side of the field. Cross a small stream and continue along the right hand side of the next field to a gate. Continue AHEAD for a few yards and turn RIGHT at the two-way marker post. Follow the track to the next two-way marker post and go STRAIGHT AHEAD on the track. Bear SLIGHTLY RIGHT when the ground begins to climb, pass to the left of

hand side of the field. Pass through a gate and follow the track HALF RIGHT. Turn LEFT at a waymark post, on the left. Follow the track through

a gate to the right of a house and head RIGHT along the access track. Follow the track through a bend to the left and pass below Noyadd Farm to the junction with a lane. Cross the lane and the stile opposite. Turn RIGHT and head along the field, then round to the LEFT. Cross a stile at the far end of the field and descend the bank to a waymark post. Head along the field to cross a stile near a fence and then continue AHEAD and round to the left to Quarry Lane.

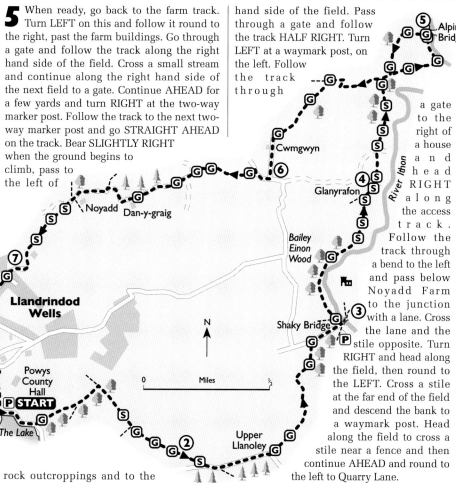

rock outcroppings and to the right of trees. At the top of the field, go through a waymarked gate on the left. Follow the track along the left hand side of the next field, passing through a gate on route. Ignore a turning to the right and continue AHEAD, with a house visible ahead. Go through a gate and turn LEFT on a lane. Follow the lane down past the house.

6 When the lane bends sharply to the left, look for a waymark post on the left. Turn RIGHT and go through a gate. Follow the track ahead, ignoring the first three gates on the left. Go through the fourth gate on the left and follow the track AHEAD. After going through the next gate, follow the track along the left

7 Turn RIGHT and follow the lane downhill. Shortly after passing an old building on the right (a former blacksmith's), go through a kissing gate on the left. Descend a short bank and head right across the grass to a road. Turn RIGHT and follow the road past the junction with a road coming from the right. At the crossroads, continue AHEAD, passing the Metropole Hotel. At the next junction, cross over and follow the driveway up towards County Hall. Take the first footpath on the right. Follow this to the left, turning RIGHT at a junction of paths. Go past an old gate and continue AHEAD to the road. Turn LEFT to return to the lake.

LLANDRINDOD WELLS WOODLAND CIRCULAR

DESCRIPTION A 5 mile walk starting from Llandrindod Lake and passing through attractive areas of woodland and fields with hill views, plus the site of a former quarry (now an attractive 'wetland' setting). Allow about 3 hours for the walk.

START Llandrindod Wells Lake, SO 063606.

I From Lakeside visitor facilities, follow the pavement around the Lake in a clockwise direction until reaching a picnic area sign on the right, near the lagoon. Cross the road and join the waymarked footpath opposite. Follow the path up the steps and then continue HALF RIGHT. Look for an information board on the left, detailing the wildlife that can be seen in the woods. Just beyond this, turn LEFT at the waymark sign and follow a path through the woods. Go through a kissing gate and continue along the path. Shortly after passing a small marker post, cross a small stream and turn RIGHT. At a nearby waymark post, take the left fork on a path to the right of the fence to reach a waymark post near a stile. Cross the stile and head HALF LEFT across the field to another waymark post. Bear HALF RIGHT and pass through a kissing gate. Take the left fork in the path and follow this to a kissing gate onto a lane.

2 Turn RIGHT and follow the lane to the junction with a road. Cross the road and follow the lane opposite. At the end of the lane, descend waymarked steps on the left into a dingle. Cross the footbridge and head up the bank to a stile. Head up the field past a telegraph pole – there are excellent 360 degree views from the top of the field. Cross a stile on the right and keep to the left hand side of the next field. Bear HALF LEFT on reaching a waymark post by the hedge on the

left. Cross a stile to the left of a gate and continue AHEAD to reach a gate onto a lane.

3 Turn LEFT on the lane, passing houses on both sides. Continue down the lane, passing an open field on the left and higher ground on the right. Look for a waymark post on the right and follow the footpath RIGHT across open ground towards a small rock outcropping. At another waymark post, bear HALF RIGHT, across open ground. Keep to the left of the stream to reach a waymarked stile. The quarry – on the right – is fenced off as a danger area, but provides attractive views of a wetland area. Continue AHEAD, to the left of the trees and the quarry, then head up a bank past a waymark post to a stile. Cross and head along the field. At the far side, bear RIGHT to reach a stile on a left, near the entrance to Noyadd.

4 Cross over the entrance track and follow the track AHEAD, passing below Noyadd. Go LEFT at the fork in the track. When the track turns right, go AHEAD through a waymarked gate and follow the track, taking right fork at the next waymark post. Continue AHEAD to a waymarked gate. Take the left fork in the track and the left (bridleway) option at the next waymark post. Go through a waymarked gate into a wood. Follow the path AHEAD and bear HALF RIGHT at the next waymark post. Cross a small stream, take the right fork and head HALF RIGHT at the next waymark post.

5 Pass through a gate and follow an old track along the left hand side of a field (divert RIGHT around boggy section). Ignore the stile on the left and continue AHEAD through a waymarked gate and along the left hand edge of the next two fields. Cross an access track and continue AHEAD to another gate. Follow the track along the right hand edge of the next two fields, skirting to left of wet areas. Ignore tracks coming from the right and keep on the current track, following this round to the left to reach a gate onto a lane.

6 Turn RIGHT in the lane and follow the lane round to the right. Look for a waymarked gate on the left. Go through this and head HALF LEFT across the field to the right hand of two gates. Continue along the left hand side of the next field to a gate onto a track. Turn RIGHT and follow the track to a lane. Cross the lane and the stile opposite and head HALF LEFT across the field towards a coppice. Cross a stile and follow the path HALF LEFT through the trees to a gate onto the road. Turn RIGHT and follow the road to Bailey Einon farm. Turn

SLIGHTLY LEFT down the field to a waymark post near gorse bushes. Follow a path through the bushes to a gate. Follow the path down the side of a dingle. At the far side of the trees, head to the left of a rock to a gate near a fence. Follow the path to a road. Cross the road and take the next section of path opposite. At the next road, cross and head RIGHT along the pavement. Look for the third section of path, between fences on the left. Follow the path round to the right and then turn LEFT through a kissing gate.

LEFT through a waymarked gate, opposite the entrance to Bailey Einon. Head up the left hand side of two fields. Cross stile at the top of the second field, turn RIGHT and cross two more stiles to reach a track.

7 Turn LEFT and follow the track around the hill, looking for a short waymark post on the left. Bear HALF LEFT at this point, crossing open ground to a waymark post to the right of trees ahead. At the waymark post, cross the track and take the right hand footpath, towards conifers. Cross a stile and follow the path through the trees. Go RIGHT at a junction of paths and cross a stile. Head

8 Continue AHEAD for a few yards to the waymark post and then head RIGHT to a stile. Follow a path along the lower edge of the field to a second stile and continue along the path to a third stile. Cross and take the wooden steps on the left. Turn RIGHT at the top and follow the path through woodland. On coming in sight of a house to the left, bear RIGHT, passing to the right of an oak tree. After a few yards, take the left fork in the path, leading up a short bank. Continue along the path towards the Lake and pass through a gate. Turn RIGHT to return to the Lakeside visitor facilities.

WYE VALLEY CIRCULAR, BUILTH WELLS

DESCRIPTION A choice of 5 or 8¾ miles. The outward route (of about 5 miles) follows a scenic riverside section of the Wye Valley Walk and then crosses adjacent countryside, by bridleway and lane, to Cilmeri. There is the option of a pub lunch and a visit to a local historical site. The return route (3¾ miles) is via footpath, lane and bridleway. Allow about 3 or 5¼ hours for the walk, according to option chosen.

START The Groe, Builth Wells, SO 042511.

PUBLIC TRANSPORT Powys bus service 48 (limited service) connects Cilmeri and Builth Wells. Cilmeri is a request stop on the Heart of Wales line, as is Builth Road, from where Powys bus service 47 (limited service) travels to Builth Wells town.

1 **Builth Wells to Cilmeri** (*5 miles*). From The Groe car park/bus stops, follow the tarmac path alongside the River Wye. Look out for the carving of the leaping salmon (the symbol of the Wye Valley Walk). Turn LEFT at the junction with the River Irfon and follow the Wye Valley Walk over a footbridge on the right. Bear RIGHT along the verge to a kissing gate. Go through and follow the right hand side of the field to return to the meeting place of the Wye and Irfon. Turn LEFT and follow the riverside path along two fields, connected by a gap. At the end of the second field, go through a gate, over a footbridge and continue to follow the river. Go through a gate and pass to the right of the grounds of 'The Rocks'. Follow the path through the wood. Continue AHEAD, taking the right fork at the junction in the path. Descend, steeply for a short distance, to pass under the Heart of Wales Railway Bridge.

2 Continue ahead, passing through a kissing gate. On leaving the wood, follow the riverside path along the field to a footbridge and gate in the far right corner. Continue alongside the river across the next two fields, connected by a gap. At the end of the second field, go through the gate and continue ahead, through a further two gates to reach an access track. Turn LEFT on the access track, away from the river. Pass a pond on the right and Dolyrerw Farm on the left. Shortly after passing the farm take an unmarked path on the right, leading towards Coed Dolyrerw wood. Just before reaching the wood, turn LEFT and follow a waymarked bridleway.

3 Follow the path through a short section of bracken (quite often flattened down or cleared by previous users) and continue along the right hand side of a small valley. When the path levels off cross another section of bracken (again this may have been flattened or cleared) keeping close to the hedgeline on the right. Eventually, pass through a gate, go AHEAD between trees and pass through a second gate onto a road.

4 Cross the road, aiming for the lane slightly to the right. Follow this down to the right of Rhosferig-Fawr farmhouse and go through two gates across the track. Continue down, turning RIGHT on reaching a railway bridge on the left. Pass through another farmyard, head LEFT over a river bridge and turn RIGHT to head up a lane. At the junction with the main road, turn RIGHT and follow the road past the Prince Llywelyn pub/restaurant to reach the monument to Prince Llywelyn on the left. There is also a well at this site, located down the steps in the far right corner of the monument area. Llywelyn ap Gruffydd, the last native Prince of Wales, was killed in battle at Cilmeri on 11th December 1282.

6 Head LEFT, past a waymark post, to a stile next to a watering trough. Head up the left hand side of the field to a waymarked gate and pass to the right of Rhosferig-Fach house. After a few yards, cross a stile on the right. Head HALF LEFT down the field to a stile giving onto the railway line. Cross the line with care and head up the opposite bank to another stile. Follow the left hand side of the field and cross a driveway by means of gates.

7 Head for the far right corner of the next field, pass through a band of conifers and cross a stile. Head HALF RIGHT across the next field to a stile in the far right corner and follow a path and stiles through a wooded area

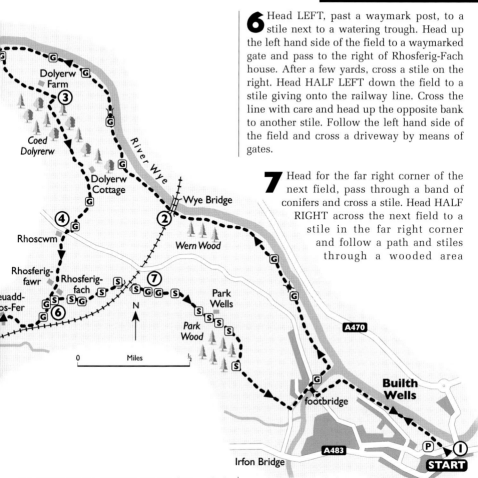

5 **Cilmeri to Builth Wells** (*3¾ miles*). Return along the main road, until reaching the 'Old Post Office' on the left. Follow the footpath sign along the driveway and over a stile on the right. Head DIAGONALLY across the field, aiming slightly to the left of the telegraph pole. Pass a marker post, follow the path through a short section of woodland and then head along the left hand side of a field to reach a stile into the churchyard. Exit the churchyard via a metal gate and head up the track to a lane. Turn LEFT to follow the lane over a bridge and turn RIGHT on the track through Neuadd-rhos-Fer farmyard and up towards Rhosferig-Fawr farm. Just after passing through a gate below the second farm, cross a stile on the right.

– skirting the edge of Park Wells house on the left. On reaching a small field, continue along the right hand edge of this, until reaching a stile on the right into woodland. Turn LEFT on the path through the woodland and continue until reaching a stile on the left, leading onto the golf course. Follow the track across the golf course (keeping an eye out for stray golf balls) to the road. Head LEFT along the road until reaching the footbridge over the River Irfon. Cross and turn LEFT to follow the tarmac path alongside the Irfon and then the Wye, to reach The Groe car park/bus stops.

ABERGWESYN COMMON & WYE VALLEY

DESCRIPTION A 9 mile walk following a quiet road (providing a view of Llysdinam house) and lane through parkland, fields and woods to open access land owned by the National Trust. It crosses a section of the open land, providing excellent views of the hills and valleys around, before descending to join the Wye Valley Walk and follow bridlepath, lane and footpaths back to the minor road near Llysdinam and then back to Newbridge-on-Wye. Allow about 5 hours for the walk.

START The Village Green, Newbridge-on-Wye. SO 016583.

PUBLIC TRANSPORT Newbridge-on-Wye is on a number of local bus routes (See Powys Travel Guide, available free from Tourist Information Centres in Powys, for general information).

1 From the Village Green, head RIGHT into Newbridge-on-Wye. Continue past the Golden Lion and turn LEFT into a side road that leads to the Rhayader to Beulah road. Cross the main road with care and head LEFT along the pavement to cross the Wye Bridge. Turn RIGHT into a side road just after the bridge.

2 Follow the minor road, past Llysdinam on the left, as it climbs gradually through parkland, then a mixture of fields and woods until reaching views of the surrounding hills. On reaching a crossroads, where the National Cycleway turns right, continue AHEAD on the lane. Pass Blaenglynolwyn farm and continue AHEAD on the bridlepath, which leads through a gate onto open access land owned by the National Trust.

3 On coming to a junction of tracks, take the track on the right. Follow the fence line on the right, until this veers right, and then continue STRAIGHT AHEAD across open ground for about three-quarters of a mile until coming in sight of a valley to the left. Cross towards the left side of the hill and gradually descend towards a path running along the lower slopes, just above the fields (there is more than one clear route through the bracken on this slope). Continue to the RIGHT along this path, to join a bridlepath section of the Wye Valley Walk, at the start of a wooded area.

4 Turn RIGHT on the Wye Valley Walk, keeping an eye out for the view of Doldowlod House (once owned by the inventor James Watt) through a gap in the trees to the left. Follow the track to the end of the National Trust land and then through farmland to reach a lane. Turn RIGHT and follow the winding lane gradually uphill until reaching a Wye Valley Walk waymark post and gate (at a point where the lane bends to the right).

5 Head along the left side of the field, cross a footbridge and gate and then head RIGHT to a second footbridge and steps. Climb the bank to a waymark post, turn LEFT to follow the stream and then head SLIGHTLY TO THE RIGHT to a gate. Continue AHEAD, keeping to the right of a fence. Cross another footbridge and take the left hand gate. Go along the right hand side of the field, cross a further footbridge and follow a short length of track to a gate. Turn LEFT and follow the track as far as the first house, then head RIGHT and across the field (keeping close to left boundary). Cross the left side of the next three fields, then cut across the middle of a further field to footbridges. Head along the right hand side of the final two fields to reach the minor road near Llysdinam. Turn LEFT, follow the road back to the Rhayader-Beulah road and retrace your steps to Newbridge-on-Wye.

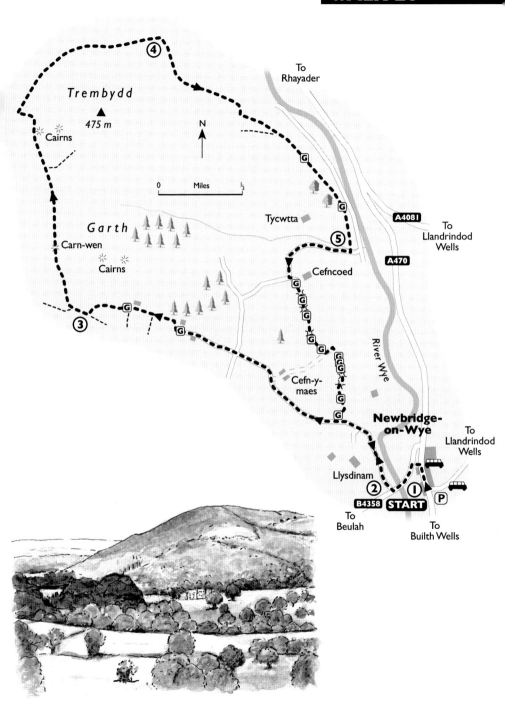

To Rhayader

Trembydd

▲
475 m

Cairns

N

0   Miles   ½

Tycwtta

A4081

To Llandrindod Wells

A470

Garth

Carn-wen

Cairns

G

④

⑤

Cefncoed

③

River Wye

Cefn-y-maes

Newbridge-on-Wye

To Llandrindod Wells

Llysdinam

② ①
B4358 START P

To Beulah

To Builth Wells

WYE, IRFON & GARTH, BUILTH WELLS

DESCRIPTION A 6½ mile walk along the scenic Wye and Irfon rivers, followed by a quiet footpath, lane and road route to Garth, a local viewpoint. The route then follows the Wye Valley Walk back to Builth Wells, passing the site of Builth Castle on the way. Allow about 3¾ hours for the walk.

START The Groe, Builth Wells, SO 043511.

PUBLIC TRANSPORT Regular services to Builth Wells from neighbouring towns, including Powys bus services 47 and 704 from Llandrindod Wells railway station

1 From the Groe, follow the Wye Valley Walk along the scenic riverside route for about ½ mile. On reaching the junction with the River Irfon, follow the tarmac path round to the left. Leave the Wye Valley Walk where it crosses a footbridge on the right. Continue AHEAD along a footpath that follows the River Irfon. Climb up the steps at the side of the Irfon Bridge and go through a gate. Cross the main road (A483) with care and enter Irfon Bridge Road opposite. Follow the road along the side of the Irfon. (The footpaths on the other side of the river are part of the grounds of Caer Beris Hotel). When the road bends to the left, cross the stile on the right. Continue alongside the Irfon, which is now less placid than the Wye and shows 'white water'. On reaching a lane, turn LEFT and continue to the junction with a minor road.

2 Cross the road and take the waymarked stile slightly to the right. Head up the left hand side of the field, cross a stile and continue along the left hand side of the next field. Cross another stile and continue along the line of an old track. At the end of the track, go through a gate on the right. Head up the left hand side of the field and go through a gate on the left. Follow the right hand side of the field and then head HALF LEFT to reach the lower (left hand) of two gates (if this is hard to open, press down on bars of the gate). Continue AHEAD to the next gate. Maintain direction over two stiles. Head HALF LEFT to a gate, cross a small stream and continue AHEAD alongside a hedge to reach a gate onto a road.

3 Follow the lane to the left. Ignore the turning the first turning on the left, for Erwhelm. At the junction, turn LEFT onto the B4520. Turn RIGHT at the next junction and then LEFT at a third junction. Pass the turning, on the right, for Maes-y-cwm. At the next junction, cross the waymarked stile ahead. Follow the gradual ascent through two gates to the trig point on Garth – *this gives excellent views of the Wye Valley, Builth Wells and the southern end of the Carneddau*. When ready, retrace the route back to the road and turn RIGHT. Follow the road towards Builth Wells.

4 On reaching a t-junction within the town, turn RIGHT and then follow the road round to the left. *A footpath sign on the left indicates the entrance to Builth Castle site, which provides additional views over the town*. The main route leads to the main road, turns left and – at the junction by the Wyeside Theatre – crosses the road and takes the first turn on the left to return to the Groe.

38

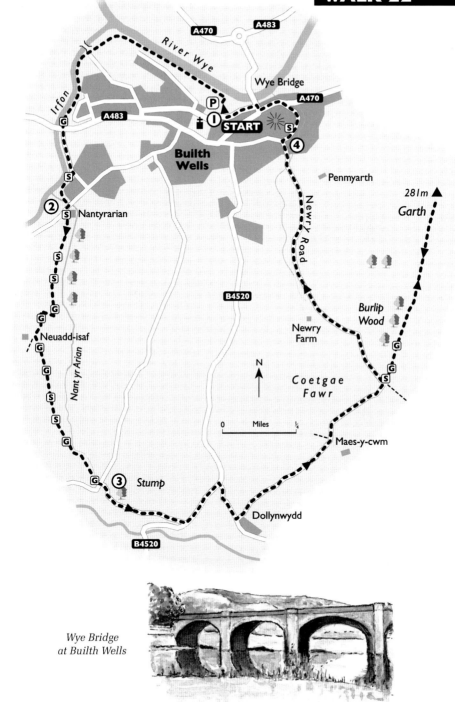

A470

A483

River Wye

Wye Bridge

A470

P

Irfon

G

A483

START

S

4

Builth Wells

Penmyarth

281m ▲

Garth

Newry Road

S

2

Nantyrarian

S

S

B4520

Newry Farm

Burlip Wood

G

Neuadd-isaf

G

G

N

Coetgae Fawr

G

S

S

Nant yr Arian

S

0   Miles   ¼

Maes-y-cwm

G

3

Stump

Dollynwydd

B4520

Wye Bridge at Builth Wells

PRONUNCIATION

These basic points should help non-Welsh speakers

Welsh	English equivalent
c	always hard, as in cat
ch	as on the Scottish word loch
dd	as th in then
f	as in of
ff	as in off
g	always hard as in got
ll	no real equivalent. It is like 'th' in then, but with an 'L' sound added to it, giving 'thlan' for the pronunciation of the Welsh 'Llan'.

In Welsh the accent usually falls on the last-but-one syllable of a word.

KEY TO THE MAPS

- Main road
- Minor road
- Walk route and direction
- ① Walk instruction
- - - - Path
- River/stream
- Ⓖ Gate
- Ⓢ Stile
- △ Summit
- Woods
- Pub
- Ⓟ Parking
- Bus service

THE COUNTRYSIDE CODE

- Be safe – plan ahead and follow any signs
- Leave gates and property as you find them
- Protect plants and animals, and take your litter home
- Keep dogs under close control
- Consider other people

Open Access
Some routes cross areas of land where walkers have the legal right of access under The CRoW Act 2000 introduced in May 2005. Access can be subject to restrictions and closure for land management or safety reasons for up to 28 days a year. Details from: www.naturalresourceswales.gov.uk.
Please respect any notices.

Published by
Kittiwake Books Limited
3 Glantwymyn Village Workshops, Glantwymyn, Machynlleth, Montgomeryshire SY20 8LY

© Text & map research: Kittiwake 2016
© Maps & illustrations: Kittiwake 2011
Drawings by Morag Perrott

Cover photos: *Main*: Towards Llandegley Rocks.
Inset: St Tecla's church, Llandegley. David Perrott

Care has been taken to be accurate.
However neither the author nor the publisher can accept responsibility for any errors which may appear, or their consequences. If you are in any doubt about access, check before you proceed.

First edition 2007. New edition 2011

Printed by Mixam UK..

ISBN: **978 1 902302 95 9**